Health Guidance Note

The Pressure Systems and Transportable Gas Containers Regulations 1989

London: HMSO

NHS Estates

An Executive Agency of the Department of Health

ISBN 0 11 321674 2

About this publication

Health Guidance Notes form an occasional series of publications prepared by NHS Estates. They respond to changes in Departmental policy or reflect changing NHS operational management, and cover specific topics.

Health Guidance Notes are intended to appraise general managers and chief executives of these changes and to offer recommendations on appropriate action. The guidance will be assimilated into the next revision of each Health Technical Memorandum, if appropriate.

The contents of this Health Guidance Note are endorsed by the NHS Management Executive for the NHS in England, the Welsh Office for the NHS in Wales, the Health and Personal Social Services Management Executive in Northern Ireland and the NHS in Scotland, Management Executive.

Health Guidance Note – 'The Pressure Systems and Transportable Gas Containers Regulations 1989'

This Health Guidance Note highlights new legislation on pressure systems and gives guidance on the implications of the Regulations.

This guidance, and references appearing within the main text, apply to England and Wales. Where references differ for Scotland and/or Northern Ireland these are given as marginal notes.

Where appropriate, marginal notes are also used to amplify the text.

Contents

1.0 Scope and application

1.1 The Pressure Systems and Transportable Gas Containers Regulations 1989 (hereafter referred to as "the Regulations") were made under the powers conferred by the Health and Safety at Work etc Act 1974 (hereafter referred to as "the 1974 Act"). Failure to comply with the requirements of the Regulations could result in legal penalties which, in the event of an incident, may include criminal proceedings against individuals.

1.2 The aim of this document is to provide management within the National Health Service with a summary of their responsibilities under the Regulations and to give guidance on their implementation.

1.3 It is not the purpose of this guidance to advise on the interpretation of the Regulations, as this is comprehensively covered in available publications (see references in section 6.0).

The Pressure Systems and Transportable Gas Containers Regulations (Northern Ireland) 1991

The Health and Safety at Work (Northern Ireland) Order 1978

2.0 Action

2.1 The requirement of the 1974 Act and the Regulations is to provide a regime, the aim of which is to ensure the safety of pressure systems.

2.2 Chief executives, general managers and managers have a duty under the 1974 Act to demonstrate that they are providing a safe working environment.

2.3 Chief executives, general managers and managers should ensure that:

   a. responsibility is delegated to a Responsible Person to implement the requirements of the Regulations;

   b. progress on implementation is monitored;

   c. their written health and safety policies reflect the requirements of the Regulations.

3.0 Introduction

3.1 This document is intended to provide guidance for chief executives, general managers and managers with regard to the implications of the Regulations. The guidance note is applicable to new and existing installations.

Background

3.2 Traditionally, pressure systems legislation in the United Kingdom has been limited to steam boilers, steam receivers and air receivers, and has focused on the vessel and not the complete pressure system.

3.3 In the late 1960s some consideration was given to the inclusion of other vessels and systems as a whole. However, this was held in abeyance until the review of health and safety legislation had been completed by a committee under the chairmanship of Lord Robens.

3.4 Following the Flixborough explosion in 1974 which involved the failure of a pressure system, a committee of enquiry proposed that similar controls to those covering steam boilers under the Factories Act should be applied to all pressurised systems. It is from this background that the Regulations developed.

The Regulations

3.5 The Regulations, which apply to steam systems and systems in which gases exert a pressure in excess of 0.5 bar above atmospheric pressure, come into force in three stages, as follows:

Operative dates	Regulation	
1 July 1990	1 Citation and commencement	*Northern Ireland 9 December 1991*
	2 Interpretation	
	3 Application and duties	
	5 Provision of information and marking	
	6 Installation	
	7 Safe operating limits	
	13 Keeping of records, etc	
	14 Application	
	15 Precautions to prevent pressurisation	
	23 Defence	
	24 Power to grant exemptions	
	25 Extension outside Great Britain	
	27 Transitional provisions (Schedule 1–6)	
1 January 1991	4* Design, construction, repairs and modification	*Northern Ireland 8 June 1992*
	16 Design, standards approval and certification	**(to the extent specified in Part 1 of Schedule 1)*
	17 Filling of containers	
	18 Examination of containers	
	19 Modification of containers	

		20 Repair work
		21 Re-rating
		22 Records
		26* Repeals, revocations and modifications

Northern Ireland 1 July 1994
*(to the extent specified in Part 1 of
Schedule 1)

1 July 1994

   4* Design, construction, repairs and modification

   8 Written scheme of examination

   9 Examination in accordance with the written scheme

  10 Action in case of imminent danger

  11 Operation

  12 Maintenance

  26* Repeals, revocations and modifications

The overall intention of the Regulations is to prevent the risk of injury from stored energy as a result of failure of a pressure system or part of it.

3.6 The Regulations cover the whole spectrum of potentially hazardous pressure systems which contain a relevant fluid rather than the few specialised vessels covered under previous legislation.

3.7 The Regulations place legal requirements on designers, manufacturers, installers, users and owners to ensure that systems are safe.

For definition of "Competent Person" see "HSC Approved Code of Practice on Safety of Pressure Systems" Regulation No 2

3.8 The introduction of the Regulations breaks new ground in the role they give to "Competent Persons". Managers are required to employ "Competent Persons" to advise on the scope of the written scheme, to draw up or certify written schemes of examination, and carry out examinations.

3.9 The Health and Safety Executive has published a leaflet giving guidance on Competent Persons with respect to the Pressure Systems and Transportable Gas Containers Regulations 1989 (see reference in section 6.0).

Health and Safety Agency for Northern Ireland

3.10 In addition, the Health and Safety Commission has published approved codes of practice which provide detailed guidance (see section 6.0). Although failure to observe the codes of practice is not in itself an offence, that failure may be taken by a court, in criminal proceedings, as proof that the Regulations have been contravened.

4.0 Management responsibilities

4.1 It is the responsibility of chief executives, general managers and managers to ensure that the premises for which they are responsible meet the requirements of all statutes.

4.2 The Regulations, unlike other health and safety legislation which broadly puts duties on the occupier or employer, put a primary duty of compliance on "users" in the case of fixed systems, and "owners" of mobile systems.

For definition of "owner" and "user" see Part 1 of the Regulations

4.3 There are circumstances where the owner's responsibilities transfer automatically to the user.

4.4 The user is defined as the employer having control of the operation of the pressure system, and this individual is therefore in the best position to ensure the system is operated in a safe manner. In the NHS this would normally be the general manager or chief executive.

Duties under the Regulations

4.5 Certain requirements of the Regulations are already in force, and listed below are the basic requirements and their application dates with particular reference to existing systems. The duties set out below relate to the user of an installed system and the owner of a mobile system.

Safe operating limits – 1 July 1990

4.6 The user shall not operate the system or allow it to be operated unless safe operating limits have been established.

Northern Ireland 9 December 1991

Reference Regulation 7

4.7 For some small simple systems, this could be little more than the establishment of a maximum operating pressure, but systems may be limited by additional parameters such as flow rate, temperature, etc. These safe operating limits must be supported by written statements and also by marking the system in a legible and durable style.

4.8 Where limits are already laid down and experience provides adequate evidence that they are safe, the existing limits may be taken as the safe operating limits. Only in cases where there is little or no evidence will a detailed assessment be necessary. If safe limits are not known and the user/owner does not have the level of technical expertise required to set them, an organisation which is competent to carry out the task should be used.

Documentary records – 1 July 1990

4.9 The user of an installed system shall keep adequate records.

Northern Ireland 9 December 1991

Reference Regulations 11, 12 and 13

4.10 Documents relating to the safety of relevant pressure systems must be kept secure and be easily accessible. These will include Competent Persons' reports, design information, records and information on modifications and repairs, and all documents relating to the establishment of safe operating limits.

4.11 Effective maintenance of relevant systems is a key requirement of the Regulations; therefore, records of maintenance programmes should be retained. This will include permit-to-work certificates where this discipline is implemented.

4.12 From 1 July 1994, documents detailed in the written scheme of examination, including the last report made by the Competent Person and any other documents which relate to the safety of the system, must be retained.

4.13 The records should be kept at the site where the pressure system is installed. If the user cannot guarantee security of records, storage at another site is permitted with the prior permission of the local Health and Safety Inspectorate.

The written scheme of examination – 1 July 1994

Reference Regulation 8

4.14 The user shall not allow a pressure system to be operated unless a written scheme for the periodic examination of the pressure system has been drawn up and certified as being suitable by a Competent Person in accordance with the Regulations.

4.15 Every relevant system will require individual assessment which will dictate future statutory inspection intervals, and will form the basis of the written scheme.

4.16 The Competent Person must certify the written scheme as being suitable for the system. Because of the type of experience required, with access to independent testing facilities and guaranteed independence from the user/owner, it is unlikely that the Competent Person will be available "in-house"; therefore, the Competent Person would normally be contracted from an established pressure systems inspection organisation.

4.17 The responsibility for defining the scope of the written scheme lies with the user. For healthcare premises, the user should produce a schematic diagram of each relevant system, which may be broken down into sub-systems if necessary. The schematic diagrams should identify and schedule all safety devices, relevant pressure vessels, pipelines and necessary pipework. The extent of pipework to be included depends on many factors, and the advice of the Competent Person should be sought. Appendix 2 of the Guidance on Regulations, produced by the Health and Safety Executive, gives typical details to be covered in the scheme.

Operation – 1 July 1994

Reference Regulation 11

4.18 The user of an installed system shall provide for any operator, adequate and suitable instruction for the safe operation of the system and the action to be taken in the case of an emergency.

4.19 There is a duty to provide adequate training to ensure the safe operation of the system. Written emergency instructions should be kept up to date.

Maintenance/repair – 1 July 1994

Reference Regulation 12

4.20 The user of an installed system shall ensure that the system is properly maintained in good repair, so as to prevent danger.

4.21   The process of repair/maintenance must not render any part of the remaining system dangerous. An employer must ensure that any adaptation or repair is carried out by persons competent to do so.

Examination – 1 July 1994

4.22   The user shall ensure that those parts of the pressure system included in the scheme of examination are examined by a Competent Person within the intervals specified in the written scheme.

Reference Regulation 9

4.23   The user of a system must ensure that those parts of the system that require examination under the written scheme are examined on or before the due date. It is the duty of the owner to ensure that adequate preparations are made enabling the Competent Person to safely examine the system.

Design/Installation – 1 July 1990 and 1 July 1994

4.24   The user shall ensure that design standards, approval and certification comply with the Regulations.

Northern Ireland 9 December 1991 and 1 July 1994

Reference Regulations 4, 5, 6 and 16

4.25   Designers are required to design for safety in specifying suitable materials and protective devices. In addition, the system must be so designed to allow access for maintenance and examination without danger.

4.26   The employer of a person who modifies or repairs a pressure system or transportable gas container at work must ensure that nothing about the way in which it is modified or repaired gives rise to danger or otherwise impairs the operation of any protective device or inspection facility.

5.0 Management action

5.1 Managers should ensure that the Regulations are brought to the attention of all who need to know about them. This may require staff training.

Existing systems

5.2 It should be ensured that:

a. installed and mobile systems which fall within the Regulations are identified;

b. safe operating limits for each system or part of a system are established and recorded, and the system labelled;

c. secure documentary records relating to each pressure system which qualifies under the Regulations are maintained;

d. a schematic diagram of each installed system is produced;

e. with the aid of the schematic diagram referred to in clause 5.2(d), a written scheme for the examination of all protective devices, pressure vessels, pipelines and pipework that may give rise to danger if a defect occurred, is drawn up and certified before 1 July 1994;

f. the systems are properly maintained.

New systems

5.3 It should be ensured that:

a. there is liaison between manufacturers, installers and engineering consultants to effect proper handover documentation and written schemes of examination for all new systems. Manufacturers and suppliers are obliged to make available the necessary documentation with all relevant plant and equipment;

b. where extensions are being made to existing pressure systems, the Responsible Person shall ensure that the complete system complies with the Regulations;

c. there is co-operation between designers, manufacturers, importers, suppliers and installers to provide safe systems in accordance with the Regulations;

d. suitable Competent Persons are appointed to certify written schemes of examination, in accordance with the guidance given in the approved code of practice;

e. where standard documentation is used, any necessary modifications are made to provide for the requirements of the Regulations.

6.0 Other reference material

The following documents, available through HMSO, are also relevant:

The Pressure Systems and Transportable Gas Containers Regulations 1989 (SI 2169: 1989)   ISBN 0 11 098169 3

A Guide to the Pressure Systems and Transportable Gas Containers Regulations 1989   *Health and Safety Executive*   ISBN 0 11 885516 6

Safety of Pressure Systems – Approved Code of Practice   *Health and Safety Commission*   ISBN 0 11 885514 X

Safety of Transportable Gas Containers – Approved Code of Practice   *Health and Safety Commission*   ISBN 0 11 885515 8

The Health and Safety at Work etc Act 1974

Pressure Systems and Transportable Gas Containers Regulations (NI) 1991 – Approved Code of Practice (HSA(63))   *Health and Safety Agency (NI)*

"Introducing Competent Persons" – Pressure Systems and Transportable Gas Containers Regulations 1989   *Health and Safety Executive* IND(S)29(L) (Obtainable from the Health and Safety Executive public enquiry point, Broad Lane, Sheffield S3 7HQ. Telephone 0742 892346)

7.0 Further information

Enquiries about this Guidance Note should be addressed to:

- (England)
  NHS Estates
  Department of Health
  1 Trevelyan Square
  Leeds LS1 6AE
  Telephone 0532 547000

- (Wales)
  Welsh Health CSA
  Heron House
  35–43 Newport Road
  Cardiff CF2 1SB
  Telephone 0222 471234

- (Scotland)
  National Health Service in Scotland
  Management Executive
  The Scottish Office
  St Andrew's House
  Edinburgh EH1 3DG
  Telephone 031–244 2080

- (Northern Ireland)
  Estate and Property Division
  Estate Services Directorate
  HPSS Management Executive
  Stoney Road
  Dundonald
  Belfast BT16 0US
  Telephone 0232 520025

About NHS Estates

NHS Estates is an Executive Agency of the Department of Health and is involved with all aspects of health estate management, development and maintenance. The agency has a dynamic fund of knowledge which it has acquired during 30 years of working in the field. Using this knowledge NHS Estates has developed products which are unique in range and depth. These are described below.

NHS Estates also makes its experience available to the field through its consultancy services.

Enquiries should be addressed to: NHS Estates, 1 Trevelyan Square, Boar Lane, Leeds LS1 6AE. Tel: 0532 547000.

Some other NHS Estates products

Activity DataBase – a computerised system for defining the activities which have to be accommodated in spaces within health buildings. *NHS Estates*

Design Guides – complementary to Health Building Notes, Design Guides provide advice for planners and designers about subjects not appropriate to the Health Building Notes series. *HMSO*

Estatecode – user manual for managing a health estate. Includes a recommended methodology for property appraisal and provides a basis for intergration of the estate into corporate business planning. *HMSO*

Capricode – a framework for the efficient management of capital projects from inception to completion. *HMSO*

Concode – outlines proven methods of selecting contracts and commissioning consultants. Both parts reflect official policy on contract procedures. *HMSO*

Works Information Management System – a computerised information system for estate management tasks, enabling tangible assets to be put into the context of servicing requirements. *NHS Estates*

Option Appraisal Guide – advice during the early stages of evaluating a proposed capital building scheme. Supplementary guidance to Capricode. *HMSO*

Health Building Notes – advice for project teams procuring new buildings and adapting or extending existing buildings. *HMSO*

Health Facilities Notes – debate current and topical issues of concern across all areas of healthcare provision. *HMSO*

Health Guidance Notes – an occasional series of publications which respond to changes in Department of Health policy or reflect changing NHS operational management. Each deals with a specific topic and is complementary to a related Health Technical Memorandum. *HMSO*

Encode – shows how to plan and implement a policy of energy efficiency in a building. *HMSO*

Firecode – for policy, technical guidance and specialist aspects of fire precautions. *HMSO*

Nucleus – standardised briefing and planning system combining appropriate standards of clinical care and service with maximum economy in capital and running costs. *NHS Estates*

Concise – software support for managing the capital programme. Compatible with Capricode. *NHS Estates*

Items noted "HMSO" can be purchased from HMSO Bookshops in London (post orders to PO Box 276, SW8 5DT), Edinburgh, Belfast, Manchester, Birmingham and Bristol or through good booksellers.

Enquiries about NHS Estates should be addressed to: NHS Estates, Marketing and Publications Unit, Department of Health, 1 Trevelyan Square, Boar Lane, Leeds LS1 6AE.

NHS Estates consultancy service

Designed to meet a range of needs from advice on the oversight of estates management functions to a much fuller collaboration for particularly innovative or exemplary projects.

Enquiries should be addressed to: NHS Estates Consultancy Service (address as above).

Printed in the United Kingdom for HMSO
Dd 297553 C23 11/93 17434